To Dad and Mom.

From: Nora

Thank you for everything.
especcially for my passport.

I love you all

Nora.

Cronin

KAZAKHSTAN

KAZAKHSTAN

Prepared by
Geography Department

Lerner Publications Company
Minneapolis

Series editors: Mary M. Rodgers, Tom Streissguth,
    Colleen Sexton
Photo researcher: Bill Kauffmann
Designer: Zachary Marell

Our thanks to the following for their help in preparing
and checking the text of this book: Dr. Craig ZumBrun-
nen, Department of Geography, University of Washington;
Dr. Larry Moses, Department of Uralic and Altaic Studies,
Indiana University.

Terms in **bold** appear in a glossary that starts on page 53.

LIBRARY OF CONGRESS CATALOGING-IN-PUBLICATION DATA

Kazakhstan / prepared by Geography Department, Lerner
    Publications Company.
        p. cm. — (Then & now)
    Includes index.
    Summary: Discusses the topography, location, ethnic mix-
ture, history and current political climate of the former
Soviet republic of Kazakhstan.
    ISBN 0-8225-2815-0 (lib. bdg.)
    1. Kazakhstan—Juvenile literature. [1. Kazakhstan.] I.
Lerner Publications Company. Geography Dept. II. Series:
Then & now (Minneapolis, Minn.)
DK903.66.K29 1993
958′.45—dc20   92-33082
                                                    CIP
                                                    AC

Manufactured in the United States of America
1 2 3 4 5 6 98 97 96 95 94 93

Pronunciation Guide

Akmola	AHK-mah-lah
Alma-Ata	AHL-mah—ah-TAH
Altai	AHL-ty
glasnost	GLAZ-nost
Kalmyk	KAHL-meek
Kyrgyz	keer-GEEZ
Nazarbayev	nah-zar-BAY-ehv
Tenghiz	ten-GEEZ
Vernyi	VAIRN-yee

• CONTENTS •

Skilled horse riders are among the most respected professionals in Kazakhstan.

"We want to enter the democratic world like any other state."

Nursultan Nazarbayev,
President of Kazakhstan

In 1992, the Soviet Union would have celebrated the 75th anniversary of the revolution of 1917. During that revolt, political activists called **Communists** overthrew the czar (ruler) and the government of the **Russian Empire.** The revolution of 1917 was the first step in establishing the 15-member **Union of Soviet Socialist Republics (USSR).**

The Soviet Union stretched from eastern Europe across northern Asia and contained nearly 300 million people. Within this vast nation, the Communist government guaranteed housing, education, health care, and lifetime employment. Communist leaders told farmers and factory workers that Soviet citizens owned all property in common. The new nation quickly **industrialized**, meaning it built many new factories and upgraded existing ones. It also modernized and enlarged its farms. In addition, the USSR created a huge, well-equipped military force that allowed it to become one of the most powerful nations in the world.

In Alma-Ata, the capital of Kazakhstan, people gathered in 1988 to watch parades that marked the anniversary of the Russian Revolution of 1917.

Wild horses graze on nutritious grasses at a nature preserve not far from Alma-Ata.

Kazakhstan, a large territory in central Asia, had been brought into the Russian Empire in the 18th century. Russian settlers moved into the area, building towns, fortresses, and Orthodox Christian churches. Most of the Kazakh people, who followed the Islamic religion, made their living by herding livestock. Kazakh towns profited from trading caravans that passed between Asia, the Middle East, and Europe. In the 19th century, new cities developed along railroad lines that linked Russia and central Asia.

After the revolution of 1917, the Soviet government established the **Kazakh Soviet Socialist Republic** and moved heavy industries into the area.

To increase the USSR's yields of wheat and corn, the Soviets also began to cultivate Kazakhstan's extensive **steppes** (grasslands). For several decades, the production of grain and heavy machinery dominated the Kazakh economy.

By the early 1990s, the Soviet Union was in a period of rapid change and turmoil. The central government had mismanaged the economy, which was failing to provide goods. To control the various ethnic groups within the USSR, the Communists had long restricted many freedoms. People throughout the vast nation were dissatisfied.

Several of the republics were seeking independence from Soviet rule—a development that worried some old-style Communists. In August 1991, these conservative Communists tried to use Soviet military forces to seize power in a **coup d'état.** Their effort failed and hastened the breakup of the USSR.

Kazakhstan's president, Nursultan Nazarbayev, strongly opposed the coup. After the breakup of the Soviet Union, Kazakhstan declared its independence and joined the **Commonwealth of Independent States**, an association of former Soviet republics. In March 1992, Kazakhstan was admitted to the **United Nations.**

Although it has won independence, Kazakhstan faces an uncertain future. Many **ethnic Kazakhs** favor returning to the country's Islamic traditions. With **ethnic Russians** forming a majority of the population, however, Kazakhstan may suffer conflict within its borders. In addition, non-Communist political parties, such as the Islamic organization Alash, are contesting Nazarbayev's hold on the Kazakh government. These parties, which seek to make sweeping social and economic changes, form a strong opposition group. Kazakhstan's future depends on cooperation within the government and in Kazakh society.

A Kazakh vendor sells popcorn balls at a market in the capital.

CHAPTER ONE

The Land and People of Kazakhstan

The Republic of Kazakhstan covers 1 million square miles (2.6 million square kilometers) in central Asia. The country stretches 1,056 miles (1,700 km) from north to south and 1,864 miles (3,000 km) from east to west. As large as all of western Europe, Kazakhstan is almost two times the size of the state of Alaska.

Kazakhstan has no outlets to the oceans, although it touches the Caspian Sea in the southeast and the Aral Sea in the south. To the north, Kazakhstan shares a long border with Russia. Lying south of Kazakhstan are the central Asian republics of Turkmenistan, Uzbekistan, and Kyrgyzstan. To the east is China.

At Atirau (formerly Guryev)—where the Ural River flows into the Caspian Sea—a woman collects water for cooking and drinking.

• Topography and Climate •

Kazakhstan's territory includes steppes, deserts, plains, and mountain ranges. In the west are the Mugodzhary Hills, an extension of Russia's Ural Mountains. The hills rise above the Caspian and Turanian lowlands, which border the northern shores of the Caspian and Aral seas, respectively. To the northeast, rolling hills and steppes stretch along Kazakhstan's border with Russia.

The Kyrgyz Steppe and the Kazakh Plateau—Kazakhstan's largest regions—extend across the center of the country. The open grasslands of these areas, which average 3,000 feet (914 meters) in elevation, are ideal for raising cattle and horses.

Plateaus, deserts, and salt basins lie south of the Kyrgyz Steppe. The Ustyurt Plateau, between the Caspian and Aral seas, crosses Kazakhstan's border with Uzbekistan. East of the Aral Sea is the Muyunkum Desert and the Betpak-Dala, a flat salt basin that is 300 miles (483 km) wide. Smaller salt basins exist south and east of Lake Balkhash, a long, narrow lake that contains both salt water and fresh water.

The mountains of eastern and southeastern Kazakhstan are high enough to sustain glaciers (permanent, slow-moving ice masses). The Altai and Tien ranges, near the Chinese border, include several peaks that reach 13,000 feet (3,962 m). Khan-Tengri, which straddles the border of Kazakhstan and Kyrgyzstan in the Tien Mountains, rises to 20,990 feet (6,398 m).

Kazakhstan's climate varies widely. In general, the north is colder than the south. Temperatures range from −40° F (−40° C) in the winter in the northern hills to 113° F (45° C) in the deserts in the summer. The basins and deserts have the greatest temperature extremes. Highlands and valleys in eastern Kazakhstan have more moderate weather.

(Above) *Cattle feed on spring pastures in the Kustanai region of northern Kazakhstan.* (Below) *The Tien Mountains, which lie in the eastern part of the country, reach heights of 13,000 feet (3,962 meters) in some places.*

A *lone rider journeys through the southeastern highlands, which get heavy snowfall in the winter months.*

Alma-Ata, the capital, averages 16° F (−9° C) in January, the coldest month, and 73° F (23° C) in July, the warmest month.

Most of Kazakhstan receives little precipitation. The desert regions of the south average about 4 inches (10 centimeters) of rain every year. The northern steppes get about 10 inches (25 cm), and about 21 inches (53 cm) of rain and snow fall per year near the highlands of the southeast. Areas of permafrost (permanently frozen ground) exist in some mountain regions.

• Rivers and Lakes •

Three major river systems in Kazakhstan provide much of the water used for agriculture and industry. In the west, the Ural and Emba rivers flow south from the Ural Mountains, across the Caspian Lowlands, and into the Caspian Sea. In the east and southeast, several rivers originate in the highlands near Kazakhstan's boundaries with Kyrgyzstan and China. The Syr Darya (River) begins in the Tien Mountains and eventually reaches the Aral Sea. The river is fed by freshwater glaciers but becomes salty along the lower half of its course. The Chu River travels along the border with Kyrgyzstan and evaporates in the Betpak-Dala. The Ili and Ayaguz rivers flow down from the mountains and into Lake Balkhash in eastern Kazakhstan.

In northern Kazakhstan are the Irtysh, the Ishim, and the Tobol rivers. After crossing into Russia, these tributaries of the Ob River eventually reach the Arctic Ocean. Under the Soviet government, engineers made plans to divert these north-flowing rivers to the south so that their waters could be used in Kazakhstan. The cost of the diversion—as well as fears that the change would affect the earth's climate—led to the cancellation of the project.

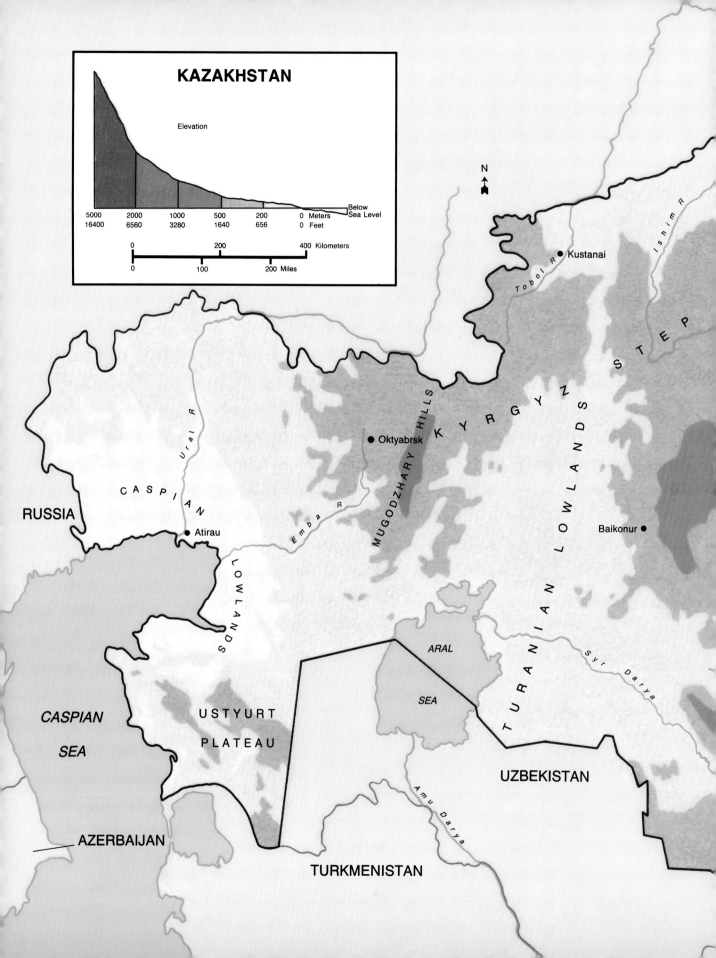

KAZAKHSTAN

Elevation

| 5000 | 2000 | 1000 | 500 | 200 | 0 | Meters | Below |
| 16400 | 6560 | 3280 | 1640 | 656 | 0 | Feet | Sea Level |

0   200   400 Kilometers

0   100   200 Miles

N

Kustanai

Tobol R

Ishim R

Ural R

Oktyabrsk

MUGODZHARY HILLS

KYRGYZ STEP

Emba R

CASPIAN

RUSSIA

Atirau

TURANIAN LOWLANDS

Baikonur

Syr Darya

LOWLANDS

USTYURT

PLATEAU

ARAL

SEA

CASPIAN

SEA

UZBEKISTAN

AZERBAIJAN

Amu Darya

TURKMENISTAN

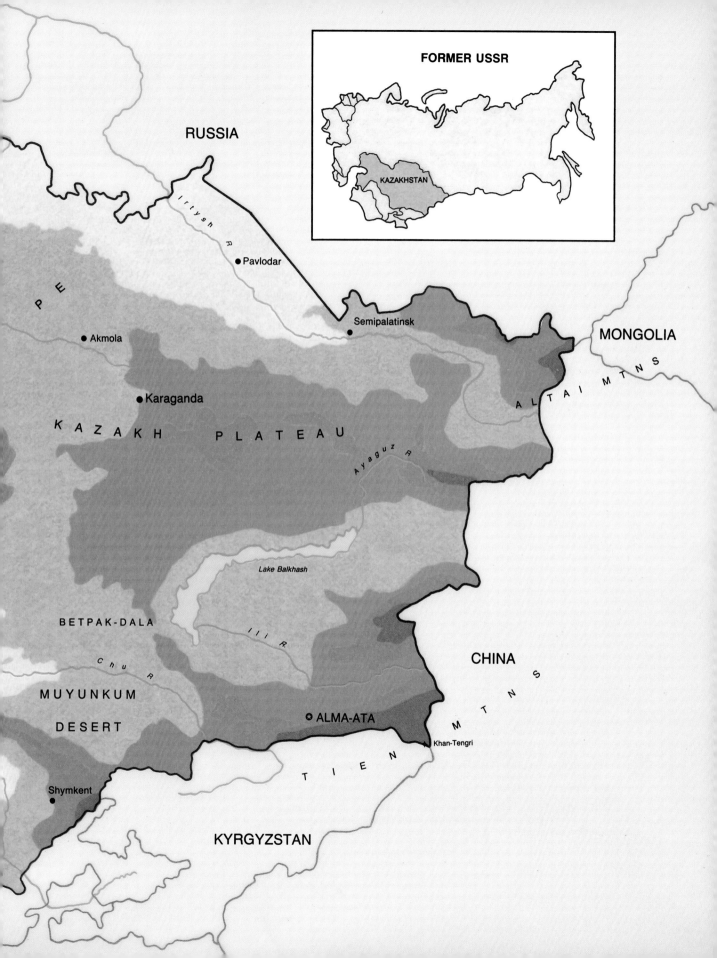

Kazakhstan has nearly 50,000 lakes, most of which are less than 1 square mile (2.59 square km) in size. For much of the year, the smaller lakes either evaporate or become marshy bogs. Lakes in the lowlands and deserts are salty, while those in the northern steppes and in the mountains have fresh water. Farmers use the waters of Lake Balkhash for irrigation during the spring and summer months.

The Aral Sea is a saltwater lake that lies in both Kazakhstan and Uzbekistan. The dumping of fertilizers, chemicals, and wastes from irrigation systems and factories has caused severe pollution in the lake and in the surrounding area. Almost half of the people living near the Aral Sea suffer from illnesses

In the spring, melting snow swells the streams and rivers that flow from the mountains to lowland areas of Kazakhstan.

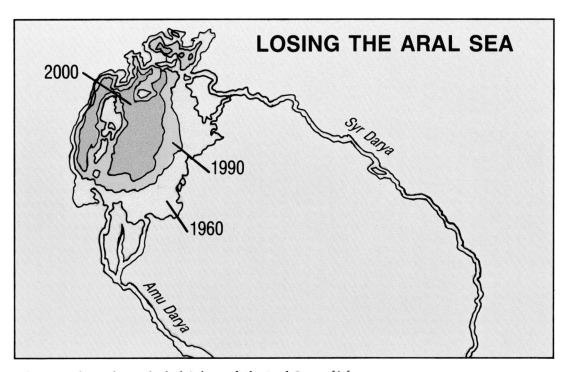

This map shows the gradual shrinkage of the Aral Sea, which crosses the border between Uzbekistan and Kazakhstan. To irrigate farmland in these republics, the Soviets rerouted the waters of the Amu Darya and the Syr Darya, the Aral's main sources of inflowing water. The loss of river water and evaporation have caused the Aral to shrink.

Located high in the mountains near Alma-Ata, the Medeo sports complex boasts the world's fastest skating rink. Since the rink's completion in the 1950s, international athletes have broken more than 100 world records on its surface, which is 437 yards (400 m) long.

caused by poisons in the air and water. In addition, the drawing of water from rivers that feed the lake is causing it to shrink. Experts believe the Aral Sea may disappear completely in about 30 years.

• Cities •

Kazakhstan had few large cities before the 20th century. Most of the population lived in movable tents, called yurts, or in small agricultural or trading villages. Russian settlements grew in the 19th century along railroad lines that linked central Asia with the rest of the Russian Empire. The arrival of ethnic Russian industrial workers caused rapid growth in Kazakhstan's cities after World War II (1939–1945). Fifty-eight percent of the population now lives in urban areas.

Alma-Ata (population 1.1 million), the capital of Kazakhstan, occupies an oasis (fertile area) at the foot of the Tien Mountains. The name Alma-Ata means "father of apples" and refers to the extensive apple orchards that grow in the surrounding region. The city was founded in 1855 as the Russian fortress of Vernyi. In the early 20th century, after an important railway was built nearby, Alma-Ata expanded.

The majority of Alma-Ata's people are industrial workers from Russia and Ukraine. The city's factories process tobacco and lumber and manufacture heavy machinery. A university, an academy of sciences, museums, and theaters have made Alma-Ata the cultural center of Kazakhstan.

Karaganda (population 614,000) is a northern industrial city with nearby coal mines and steel plants. With a population of 322,000, Shymkent (formerly Chimkent) is the hub of a mining region in the south and supports lead and chemical works and fruit canneries. Lying on the Irtysh River, Semipalatinsk (population 334,000) has food-processing plants, as well as leather, textile, and lumber factories. Pavlodar (population 337,000), in northeastern Kazakhstan, is a center of open-pit coal mining for powering nearby electric stations.

Copper, gold, and bauxite (raw aluminum) mines near Akmola (population 277,000) in northern Kazakhstan supply metal-finishing operations in the city. Workers in Akmola (formerly Tselinograd) also make farm machinery and process meat and grain. Northeast of the Aral Sea is Baikonur, the center of the former Soviet space program.

The architecture of downtown Alma-Ata reflects the capital's growth from a small village to a modern city of more than one million inhabitants.

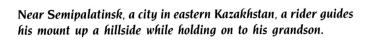

Near Semipalatinsk, a city in eastern Kazakhstan, a rider guides his mount up a hillside while holding on to his grandson.

Kazakh and Russian workers share a joke at a factory that produces ceramic tea services.

• **Ethnic Heritage** •

Kazakhstan has three distinct settlement zones. Ethnic Kazakhs populate the southern and western regions of the country. In the steppes and plains of the north and northeast, the inhabitants are generally **ethnic Slavs** (Russians and Ukrainians). This zone includes most of the country's big cities. Slavs and many other ethnic groups live in central Kazakhstan.

The modern Kazakhs emerged in the 16th century, when a large group of Turkic-speaking peoples broke away from the rule of eastern Asian Mongols. In the 18th century, while suffering a series of invasions from China, the Kazakhs allied with the growing Russian Empire to strengthen their defenses. Russians later moved into the area to build forts, towns, and railroads.

Although the ethnic Kazakhs now have their own independent state, many still live outside their homeland. About 6.5 million Kazakhs inhabit Kazakhstan, making up 38 percent of the country's population of 16.9 million. Kazakhstan also is home to 6.2 million Russians and to 1 million Ukrainians. Together, they form 43 percent of the population. The country also has 900,000 Germans and large groups of Uzbeks, Tatars, and Koreans.

Kazakhstan's large Slavic population poses a challenge for the country. Many leaders favor Kazakh, rather than Russian, as the nation's official language. Kazakh society is also turning to the Islamic traditions that dominated central Asia before Russian settlement. Many ethnic Slavs are resisting these changes and are returning to Russia and Ukraine. As a result, Kazakhstan is losing skilled managers and laborers.

An Uzbek vendor (below) *weighs apples and plums for a Russian customer. Alma-Ata is famous for its apple orchards, which produce a fruit that can weigh as much as 18 ounces (500 grams).*

(Above) **A Kazakh Muslim (follower of the Islamic religion) says his prayers before eating a meal.** (Below) **The mausoleum (above-ground tomb) of the 12th-century Islamic poet and preacher Ahmed Yesevi lies northwest of Shymkent. Built in the late 1300s, the tomb is a sacred site for Kazakh Muslims.**

• Religion •

The religion of Islam has been a strong force in Kazakhstan ever since its arrival from the Middle East in the 8th century. In modern times, the Soviet Union suppressed all forms of religious worship, including the Eastern Orthodox faith practiced by ethnic Slavs. Many churches and mosques (Islamic houses of prayer) closed under Soviet rule. Despite the restrictions, Islam survived among the Kazakhs. Every major city in Kazakhstan has at least one large mosque, and workers are repairing mosques that the Soviets closed or damaged. New mosques are opening in small towns and villages.

Many Kazakh Muslims (followers of Islam) are pressing for the adoption of Islam as an official state religion. The republic is seeking closer economic ties with other Muslim countries, such as Iran and Turkey. In addition, the Kazakhs are expanding Islamic influence in education, in the arts, and in everyday life. Alash, a new Islamic political party, is calling for a state based strictly on Islamic religious principles.

A belief system called **Sufism** is also popular in Kazakhstan. This branch of Islam, whose members worship in private and follow holy mystics, originated in Persia (modern Iran). The Sufis of Kazakhstan see their belief as a unique form of national identity.

Non-Kazakhs living in the republic follow several non-Islamic faiths. Russians and Ukrainians are members of the Eastern Orthodox Church, a branch of Christianity. Orthodox churches exist in all of Kazakhstan's major cities. Most of Kazakhstan's Germans are members of the Lutheran Church, a Protestant Christian sect that began in Germany in the 16th century. Kazakhstan also has a small community of Jews, many of whom reside in cities. Koreans in the region follow the Buddhist faith.

• Language, Education, and Health •

Kazakh belongs to the Altaic language family, which also includes Turkish, Uzbek, and Mongolian. Although there are several dialects of Kazakh, ethnic Kazakhs from different regions of the country can usually understand one another.

Russian settlers introduced their Slavic language to Kazakhstan, but Kazakhs have generally resisted learning Russian. Few rural Kazakhs speak this tongue, which may soon be abandoned completely by the non-Slavic population. In addition, the Kazakh government may make Kazakh the official language and may replace Cyrillic—the alphabet used to write Russian—with Arabic or Latin lettering.

Prior to the 20th century, almost all schools in Kazakhstan used Kazakh to instruct their students. Religious schools from the elementary to the university level taught the principles of Islam. Students who graduated with religious degrees were employed in mosques or they interpreted and applied **Sharia**—laws based on Islam.

Religious schools gradually disappeared after Kazakhstan became a Soviet republic. In their place,

In Karaganda, children from Kazakhstan's German minority are taught in their native tongue.

Signs in Russian (near the red arrows) *and **Kazakh** direct patrons of a health resort to mineral baths and showers.*

(Above) **Although the overall life expectancy at birth for citizens of Kazakhstan is 69 years, the figure for women is 74 years and for men is 65 years.** (Below) **In Shymkent (formerly Chimkent), a five-year-old Kazakh relaxes at her home, where she lives with her parents, brothers, and grandparents.**

the Kazakh government founded secular (nonreligious) schools that taught academic subjects in Russian and Kazakh. About 90 percent of the population is now literate in either language.

Kazakhstan's students attend seven to nine years of primary school, followed by two or three years of secondary school. Universities and technical schools in Kazakhstan's cities offer advanced degrees and enroll more than 500,000 students.

Health care in the central Asian republics improved under Soviet rule, although most rural areas still lack physicians and adequate medical facilities. Pollution from factories in the cities is causing health problems among workers and residents. In addition, many Kazakhs living near the Aral Sea suffer pollution-related illnesses.

Infant mortality, or the number of babies that die within one year of birth, is 44 per 1,000 births in Kazakhstan. This figure is lower than average for other former Soviet republics in central Asia. Kazakhstan's life expectancy is 69 years, an average figure for the region.

CHAPTER TWO

Kazakhstan's Story

According to archaeologists, humans inhabited Kazakhstan as long ago as 40,000 B.C. Scientists have uncovered rock pictures, stone tools, and cave paintings in the mountains of eastern Kazakhstan. Early peoples also left "deer stones," which have distinctive carved pictures of leaping deer, and huge burial mounds called the Pazyryk Kurgans. Beginning in 1000 B.C., the nomadic peoples of Kazakhstan established a more settled way of life. They herded cattle, bred horses, and hunted with bows and arrows and iron weapons.

From 200 B.C. to 200 A.D., people known as the Hsiung-nu entered Kazakhstan from Siberia to the north and Mongolia to the east. Like the earlier population of Kazakhstan, the Hsiung-nu used horses to control their herds of cattle and sheep. After conquering the people of central Asia, some of the Hsiung-nu moved west into Russia. Those who remained were conquered in turn by new groups from Mongolia. Overpopulation, climate changes, and

At an Alma-Ata park, a cleaning woman sweeps the pavement in front of a row of statues of national heroes.

Broad burial mounds called kurgans dot the landscape of eastern Kazakhstan.

In the 1200s, the Mongol leader Batu Khan founded the Golden Horde, an empire that covered much of western Kazakhstan. The empire took its name from the color of Batu Khan's tent and from the word orda, *which means "camp."*

political turmoil made the steppes of central Asia an unproductive and violent place. During the next few centuries, many who settled in Kazakhstan later migrated from the region.

In the middle of the 6th century A.D., a powerful Turkic empire arose in Mongolia. As its leaders moved westward through central Asia and into Russia, many Turkic-speaking people settled in Kazakhstan. Trading centers arose along newly established caravan routes that passed through central Asia on their way to the Middle East.

The Turkic Empire came under frequent attack during the next 500 years. Arab armies from the south, for example, pressed as far north as the Syr Darya Valley in the 8th century. The Arabs brought the Islamic religion and built mosques in central Asia's trading hubs.

• The Mongol Empires •

In 1130, the Khitan, a Mongol people from the northeast, invaded the mountainous region east of

Lake Balkhash. A century later, Genghis Khan united several independent Mongol groups under his command and swept into Kazakhstan, Russia, and eastern Europe. After the death of Genghis Khan in 1227, his grandson Batu Khan established the empire of the Golden Horde—which covered Russia and western Kazakhstan—in 1251. In the late 13th century, eastern Kazakhstan became part of the Chagatai Empire, another Mongol realm. The Mongol leaders of central Asia eventually converted to the Islamic faith.

After suffering several defeats in the Middle East, the Mongol Empire began to weaken in the 14th century. Seeking to revive the realm of Genghis Khan, a fierce warrior named Timur (Tamerlane in Europe) marched into central Asia at the head of a huge army. After conquering much of Asia and

The nomadic peoples of Kazakhstan lived in yurts—round felt tents that were constructed on a sturdy hoop frame with interlocking poles. Roughly 60 poles were needed to complete the structure, which could be quickly dismantled and reassembled.

the Middle East, Timur founded the Timurid Empire and built his capital at Samarkand in modern Uzbekistan. But after Timur's death in 1405, the empire broke apart.

At this time, another Mongol group known as the White Horde was taking control of Kazakhstan. The White Horde eventually divided into separate realms. The strongest of these were the Nogai khanate (realm of a khan or ruler) in the west and the Uzbek khanate, which stretched eastward and southward from the Aral Sea. The Sunni sect of Islam became the dominant religion among the people of the khanates.

• Kazakh Expansion •

The ethnic Kazakhs emerged in the 1500s when a number of clans (groups of families) broke away from the Uzbek khanate and moved into the river valleys around Lake Balkhash. The name Kazakh

A *modern mosaic* (above) *in the Kazakh style depicts Mongol forces in battle.* Timur (top), *one of the most famous Mongol commanders, had a reputation for being both ruthless and scholarly.*

Descended from a mixture of central Asian peoples, Kazakhs became a distinct ethnic group in the 1500s. This present-day Kazakh wears a traditional headdress and silk clothing.

may refer to an early clan chieftain or it may describe a style of life.

Under their leader, Khan Kasym, the Kazakhs expanded across much of the territory of modern Kazakhstan. Within this area, three new hordes emerged—the Great Horde of eastern Kazakhstan, the Middle Horde in the center, and the Little Horde in the west. Various ethnic groups continued to live independently in the region.

The Kazakh hordes frequently warred among themselves and against enemies who lived along

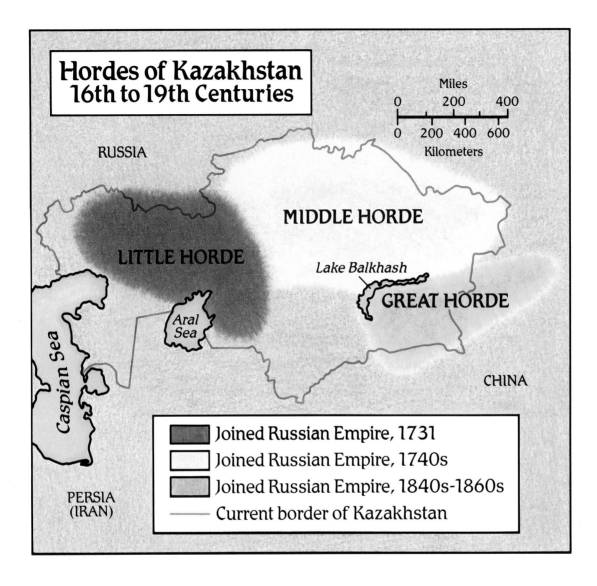

Hordes of Kazakhstan
16th to 19th Centuries

Miles

RUSSIA

MIDDLE HORDE

LITTLE HORDE

Lake Balkhash

GREAT HORDE

Aral
Sea

Caspian Sea

CHINA

Joined Russian Empire, 1731
Joined Russian Empire, 1740s
Joined Russian Empire, 1840s-1860s
Current border of Kazakhstan

PERSIA
(IRAN)

their borders. One of their strongest foes was the Russian Empire, a realm to the west and north that was ruled by a czar. Clashes often broke out between the Russians and the Kazakhs of the Little Horde. But attacks by the Kalmyks, a fierce nomadic group from western China, prompted the Little Horde to seek Russian protection. The Russians brought the Little Horde under their control in 1731. The Middle Horde merged with the Russian Empire in 1742.

In the 16th century, nomadic Kazakh clans organized into three separate groupings, called hordes. By the mid-19th century, the Little, Middle, and Great hordes had joined the Russian Empire for defensive and economic reasons.

A statue honors the Kazakh hero Amangeldy Imanov, who led an anti-Russian uprising in 1916. Imanov formed the first units of the Soviet Red Army in Kazakhstan and was killed in 1919 while battling the anti-Soviet forces of the Alash Orda.

• Russian Settlement •

By the 1840s, the czar's forces controlled the lands of the Great Horde and were pushing into northern Kazakhstan. After Russia built the fortress of Vernyi (modern Alma-Ata) in the 1850s, Russians settled in eastern Kazakhstan as far as the Chinese frontier.

Although the Russians were building new farms and cities, many Kazakhs resisted Russian rule. In the early 20th century, the czarist government also came under attack by Russian revolutionaries known as Communists. A rebel named Amangeldy Imanov led an uprising in Kazakhstan in 1916. As the revolt spread across central Asia, czarist forces lost control of the region. In 1917, the Communists succeeded in toppling the czar and establishing a Communist government in Russia.

Alma-Ata's central square sits between two administrative buildings that the Soviets constructed as offices of the Communist party.

Seeing an opportunity to gain self-rule, a popular movement of Kazakhs known as the Alash Orda fought the Communist Red Army. More than one million Kazakhs died during a civil war that lasted from 1918 to 1921. The Red Army finally defeated the Alash Orda in the early 1920s.

• *New Republics in Central Asia* •

Communist leaders extended their control to Kazakhstan by creating Communist organizations in the region. These groups were made up mostly of Russians but also included a few Kazakhs. In July 1919, the Communists founded the Kirghiz Revolutionary Committee. (At this time, the Russians called the Kazakhs by the name Kirghiz.) In 1920, the Communist government founded the **Autonomous Kirghiz Soviet Socialist Republic** (SSR). This republic joined the newly formed USSR in 1922.

Under the USSR's ruler Joseph Stalin, Soviet authorities began to change the character of Kazakh life in the late 1920s. The government seized private property and transferred it to the Communist party. Small farms were combined into state-owned **collective farms.** The government banned the herding of sheep and goats and forced Kazakhstan's nomadic peoples to join the collectives.

Stalin put in motion a plan of industrialization and modernization throughout the USSR in the 1930s. This plan improved Kazakhstan's systems of education, health care, transportation, and communication. The campaign, however, also caused a population shift in the republic. Other groups, including ethnic Germans and ethnic Slavs, came to work in Kazakhstan's newly built urban industries.

Many Kazakh leaders—both Communist and non-Communist—resisted these changes. In response, the Soviet government executed many prominent

During World War II, the western Soviet Union was invaded by the armies of Germany. Kazakh troops of the 316th Infantry Division under the command of Major General I. V. Panfilov traveled westward to help defend Moscow, the Soviet capital. This statue in Alma-Ata honors 28 Kazakh soldiers who withstood an attack by dozens of German tanks in 1941.

Under Soviet rule, agriculture and industry in Kazakhstan changed. New policies forced farmers to give their land to the state, which combined many small farms into huge collective estates. Armed guards (left) patrolled the collectives, making sure that workers remained on the job. An artwork (below) in Alma-Ata shows mining complexes and the manufacturing of metals.

Kazakhs throughout the 1930s. Russians arrived to take control of Kazakhstan's Communist government. In 1936, the Soviet government officially established the Kazakh Soviet Socialist Republic.

• World War II and Its Aftermath •

At the same time, the German leader Adolf Hitler was building up his country's armed forces and **annexing** (taking over) neighboring states. Hitler's actions led to the outbreak of World War II in 1939. Although Stalin had signed a peace treaty with Hitler, the German leader launched an attack on the western Soviet Union in June 1941.

Despite its great distance from Europe, Kazakhstan was strongly affected by World War II. The

Soviet government moved industries to central Asia to keep them safe from Germany's armies. New factories processed Kazakhstan's valuable natural resources, such as coal and iron ore. This change caused a rise in investment and production in the region.

During the war, Stalin suspected many different ethnic groups of disloyalty and exiled them to Kazakhstan. These groups included Russian Jews, ethnic Germans, Ukrainians, Tartars, and Chechen-Ingush. Many of these exiles were not allowed to return to their homes after the war.

Soviet planners increased investment in Kazakhstan's industry and agriculture in the postwar years. State-owned companies extracted precious energy and mineral resources from underground deposits in northern and eastern Kazakhstan. Factories processed raw materials, produced machinery, and prepared wool, hides, meat, fish, salt, and butter. In addition, the Soviets placed nuclear weapons throughout the republic.

After the war ended, the Soviets expanded agriculture in Kazakhstan. During the 1950s, Kazakh and Russian farm workers (left) *learned how to operate new machinery on a collective dairy farm. At the same time, the Virgin Lands program was bringing huge amounts of grassland under cultivation* (above) *to grow corn, wheat, and other grains.*

In the 1950s, the Soviet leader Nikita Khrushchev introduced the Virgin Lands program to convert Kazakhstan's grasslands from pasture to farmland for crops. Harvests of grain and corn were large at first, but the plan suffered from droughts, poor growing conditions, and inadequate planning.

To solve these problems, Dinmukhmed Kunayev, a supporter of Khrushchev, was appointed secretary (leader) of the Communist party of Kazakhstan in 1959. Despite Kunayev's efforts, crop yields in the 1960s and 1970s began to drop. As a result, for the first time, the Soviet Union was forced to import grain to feed its people.

• *Gorbachev and Reform* •

Although living standards were rising in Kazakhstan, central planning of the Soviet economy led to inefficiency, corruption, and economic decline. By the early 1980s, shortages of food and consumer goods were common. Mikhail Gorbachev,

Under Soviet rule, the writing of graffiti on walls was illegal, and offenders were usually fined.

(Left) **In 1990**, *crowds of Kazakhs gathered near Semipalatinsk to oppose the testing of nuclear weapons in the area.* (Below) **Soviet president Mikhail Gorbachev** (left) **and Kazakh leader Nursultan Nazarbayev** (middle) *met in May 1991, only months before the attempted overthrow that led to the breakup of the Soviet Union and to the independence of Kazakhstan.*

who became the Soviet leader in 1985, attempted to reform the system with the new policies of **perestroika** (economic restructuring) and **glasnost** (openness).

Under glasnost, Soviet citizens were allowed to express their views more freely in Soviet media. For the first time, Kazakhstan's leaders, including Kunayev, came under harsh public criticism. Open demonstrations prompted Kunayev to resign in 1986. When the Soviets appointed a Russian, Gennadi Kolbin, to succeed Kunayev, new protests broke out in Alma-Ata. Army units used force to disperse the crowds, causing several deaths and many injuries.

In June 1989, Gorbachev attempted to calm the situation by naming Nursultan Nazarbayev, an ethnic Kazakh, to replace Kolbin. A supporter of Gorbachev, Nazarbayev favored the Soviet leader's economic and political reforms.

Gorbachev's policies worried conservative members of the Communist party. On August 19, 1991, a group of military and political leaders arrested Gorbachev and attempted to seize power. Nazarbayev opposed the coup d'état, fearing that it would lead to military action and widespread violence in Kazakhstan. Within a few days, demonstrations in

In use since mid-1992, the new flag of the Republic of Kazakh- stan flies over a building in Alma-Ata. On the blue emblem are the sun, an eagle in flight, and a vertical stripe of tradi- tional Kazakh decoration.

cities across the USSR caused the coup to collapse. Gorbachev was released, and the coup plotters were arrested.

• Independence •

The attempted coup further weakened the Soviet government, which could no longer control the movement for self-rule in the nation's republics. Within weeks, Kazakhstan and all of the other Soviet republics declared independence from the Soviet Union. Nazarbayev was reelected Kazakhstan's president in November 1991. In December 1991, the Commonwealth of Independent States was founded as an association of former Soviet repub- lics. Kazakhstan joined the commonwealth and in March 1992 was admitted to the United Nations.

After the breakup of the Soviet Union, Commu- nist leaders in Kazakhstan renamed their organiza- tion the Socialist party and began to modernize the country's economy. For example, Kazakhstan has started **joint ventures** with several foreign com- panies to explore for oil in the northwestern part of the country. The Kazakh government is also sell- ing state-owned industries to private owners and distributing land to individual farmers.

Nazarbayev plans to smooth the difficult transi- tion to an open economy by encouraging foreign investment in Kazakhstan. With its extensive farm- land and natural resources, the nation seeks to compete successfully on the world market for food, energy, and raw materials.

By allowing opposition parties, Nazarbayev also hopes to lessen criticism of his past as a Communist leader. Although Alash and other groups want to have more political power, an improving economy will help the country to avoid the civil conflict that is occurring in other former Soviet republics.

CHAPTER THREE

Making
a Living
in Kazakhstan

For centuries, the people of Kazakhstan depended on their animal herds to make a living. The Kazakhs also profited from caravan trade between Europe and Asia. During the 20th century, when the country became a Soviet republic, its economy underwent a great change. Many of Kazakhstan's cities boomed as the Soviet government moved factories into the region and began to mine the area's natural resources. By the 1980s, however, the long period of inefficient management was causing shortages of consumer goods.

Kazakhstan's leaders must now make difficult choices to create a more self-sufficient national economy. The government still owns and operates major industries, and the country has not yet ended

Milk, eggs, and other essential goods are on sale at a small open-air market in Alma-Ata. In most parts of Kazakhstan, consumer items are in short supply.

centralized planning. Only a few of the collective farms set up under Soviet rule have been disbanded. Industries that cannot compete on the world market may close, and unproductive farms will lose money. Rising unemployment among farmers and factory workers could lead to political unrest.

Shoppers line up to buy scarce loaves of bread.

To help the economy, the Kazakh government is encouraging investment from foreign countries. For example, businesses in the United States and Europe are seeking access to Kazakhstan's valuable deposits of oil and natural gas. In addition, Kazakhstan has signed trade agreements with Iran, Turkey, and Pakistan—nations that are eager to develop new markets in the central Asian republics. Kazakh leaders believe that foreign trade will be the key to their country's future prosperity.

• Manufacturing and Trade •

The Soviet government began to develop Kazakhstan's industries during World War II. After Germany invaded Russia, the Soviets moved factories into central Asia to prevent their capture

or destruction. The large cities of northern Kazakhstan—including Semipalatinsk, Akmola, and Karaganda—have since become major industrial centers. The manufacturing sector provides at least 75 percent of the jobs in Kazakhstan, mainly to Russians, Ukrainians, and Germans.

Most of Kazakhstan's factories produce materials tied to mining or farming. Agricultural fertilizers and chemicals are made for local use and for export. Foundries refine iron, copper, and aluminum ores into ingots (bars), which are then exported for use in making finished goods. Kazakhstan also produces cotton textiles, wool fabrics, leather shoes, bags, and garments. Food-processing centers furnish butter, cheese, and yogurt.

Molten metal is poured into huge vats at a plant in Karaganda, one of Kazakhstan's industrial hubs. Russians, Ukrainians, and Germans hold most of the country's manufacturing jobs.

At a ceramics factory, a worker paints a floral design on a glazed teapot.

KAZAKHSTAN'S ECONOMIC ACTIVITIES

Industry

Textiles

Building Materials

Coal

Metal Mining

Oil

Oil Refining

Hydroelectric Energy

Natural Gas

Pipeline

Dairy Cattle

Beef Cattle

Herding

Mixed Crops

Grain

Orchards

Cotton

(Left) **A worker guides a coal-digging machine at a mine in northern Kazakhstan.** (Below) **At the Tenghiz field north and east of the Caspian Sea, drillers operate a large derrick to tap deposits of crude oil.**

Almost 90 percent of Kazakhstan's trade is with Russia and with the other members of the Commonwealth of Independent States. In the future, closer economic ties with the Middle East will create new markets for Kazakhstan's products. The country's energy resources—coal, oil, and natural gas—will also bring in export earnings. The Kazakh government continues to deny rumors that it plans to sell some of its nuclear weapons to other countries to make additional foreign income.

• Mining and Energy •

Kazakhstan has many important mineral resources, including zinc, copper, lead, and bauxite. Before Kazakhstan's independence, the Soviet regime shipped most of the country's raw metal ores to Russia for the manufacture of finished goods. Little of the profit from the sale of these goods came back to Kazakhstan. The Kazakhs can now benefit from their resources by selling them—at market prices—directly to foreign countries.

Kazakhstan also possesses abundant energy resources. Coal mines exist in the northern steppes near Karaganda and in the southern region near Shymkent. A natural-gas field lies north of the Caspian Sea near Kazakhstan's border with Russia. Drillers have found deposits of crude oil, including the huge Tenghiz field, north and east of the Caspian Sea. The new Kazakh government has signed agreements with companies in Turkey, Britain, France, Italy, and the United States to develop and market Kazakhstan's extensive oil reserves.

Dams and power plants along the Irtysh River and in the mountains harness fast-flowing water to generate electricity. In addition, Kazakhstan has large, coal-powered electric plants that produce enough power for export to Russia. A nuclear power plant near the Caspian Sea continues to operate, although it is aging and inefficient. Kazakhstan's leaders must decide whether to close this plant or to modernize it with foreign assistance.

In most Kazakh cities, cars are a luxury few people can afford. As a result, most urban citizens travel by public transportation. Here, a bus powered by electricity makes its way along tramlines in Alma-Ata.

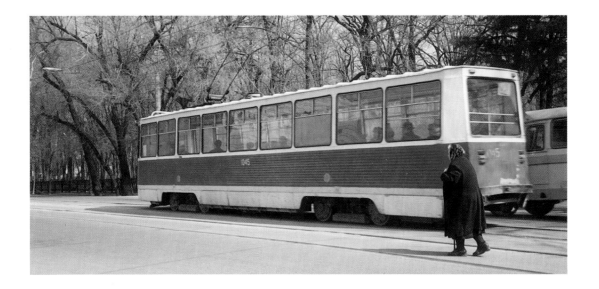

• *Agriculture and Fishing* •

Most of the agricultural workers in Kazakhstan are ethnic Kazakhs. The country's farmers produce food crops—such as fruit, rice, corn, and wheat—or raise cattle and sheep for their hides, meat, and milk. Many herders still move with their flocks between winter and summer pastures. Kazakhstan has exported meat, grain, and fruit for many years, mostly to Russia.

As the Kazakh government disbands collective farms, the land and animals are being divided among the former collective workers or are being sold to farmers. New, private farms are quickly increasing the supply of meat, as Kazakh farmers take advantage of open markets to sell their livestock at a profit.

Kazakh farmers have grown cotton, an important export crop, for centuries. Under the Soviet government, irrigation systems and the use of fertilizers increased cotton yields. These methods, however, resulted in serious environmental damage to soil and waterways.

Environmental abuse also caused the decline of Kazakhstan's fishing industry. Around the Aral Sea, for example, catches dropped rapidly as irrigation depleted the rivers feeding into the sea. As the sea shrunk, fishing fleets were stranded, and villages that were once on the Aral's shores had to be abandoned. By 1992, the Aral's fishing industry was out of business, a change that forced the closure of many fish-processing plants in the region.

The Caspian Sea, however, still supplies annual catches of fish that factories freeze or can for the local market. A major exportable fish food is caviar, which comes from the eggs of Caspian sturgeon. Increased pollution flowing into the Caspian and decreasing water levels are endangering Kazakhstan's hauls of sturgeon.

Yellow and red apples line the tables at a market in Alma-Ata, whose name means "father of apples" in the Kazakh language.

Kazakhstan's herds of livestock provide urban shoppers with a wide variety of meats, from the choicest pieces to the less expensive organ cuts.

Despite pollution and low yields, Kazakh fishing crews continue to search the waters of the Caspian Sea for valuable sturgeon, whose eggs can be processed into caviar, a high-priced hors d'oeuvre.

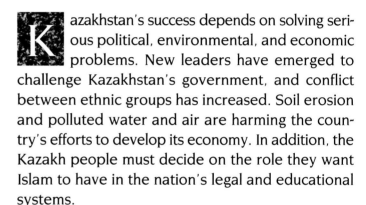
What's Next for Kazakhstan?

K azakhstan's success depends on solving serious political, environmental, and economic problems. New leaders have emerged to challenge Kazakhstan's government, and conflict between ethnic groups has increased. Soil erosion and polluted water and air are harming the country's efforts to develop its economy. In addition, the Kazakh people must decide on the role they want Islam to have in the nation's legal and educational systems.

Kazakhstan will need new trading partners to develop its wealth of natural resources. In April 1992, for example, Kazakh leaders signed agreements on economic cooperation with Kyrgyzstan, Turkmenistan, and Uzbekistan. Of concern to many foreign governments, however, are the continuing rumors that Kazakhstan plans to export its nuclear weapons to earn additional income. After years of domination by Soviet rulers, Kazakhstan and its

An elderly Russian waits to board a train in the capital. Many skilled Russian managers and professionals are leaving Kazakhstan, fearing that new governmental policies could make them second-class citizens.

central Asian neighbors are turning their economies toward the outside world.

To make meaningful reforms, the Kazakh government also must have the trust of the country's people. But Kazakhstan's current leaders, including President Nursultan Nazarbayev, are former members of the Communist party. This ruling elite is opposed by many Kazakhs, who see Nazarbayev's government as too closely linked with the old Soviet regime.

Small businesses, such as the fast-food restaurant where this young Russian works, have sprung up throughout Kazakhstan since independence.

FAST FACTS ABOUT KAZAKHSTAN

Total Population	16.9 million
Ethnic Mixture	38 percent Kazakh 37 percent Russian 6 percent Ukrainian 5 percent German
CAPITAL and Major Cities	ALMA-ATA, Karaganda, Shymkent, Akmola, Semipalatinsk
Major Languages	Kazakh, Russian
Major Religion	Islam (Sunni branch)
Year of inclusion in USSR	1936
Status	Fully independent state; member of Commonwealth of Independent States since December 1991; member of United Nations since March 1992

THE STURGEON SAGA

Sturgeons are large freshwater fish that live in the Caspian Sea, where fishing crews catch them in great numbers. Even more valuable than the sturgeons' flesh are their eggs, which can be processed into an expensive appetizer called caviar.

The Soviet government once regulated the caviar industry by licensing fishing fleets and by monitoring the number of fish caught. In the 1990s, four newly independent states along the Caspian's shores—Kazakhstan, Russia, Azerbaijan, and Turkmenistan—took over the caviar business. The end of Soviet control left the industry without a single overseeing authority. As a result, poachers (illegal hunters) have been able to take unlimited amounts of sturgeon, and stocks of the fish are declining.

Overfishing is the latest in a long line of dangers that threaten the sturgeons in the Caspian Sea. Since the 1930s, hydroelectric dams that the Soviets

built on the inflowing Volga River have caused the sea's water level to drop. This decline reduces the area available to the fish for laying their eggs. The heavily polluted Volga brings in wastes from Russian factories that further endanger the sturgeons' habitat. Oil producers drill off shore, a practice that has resulted in oil spills. Mining companies block off and drain areas of the Caspian to search for mineral deposits on the sea bottom. All of these actions have made it difficult for sturgeons to survive and reproduce. Recognizing the dangers posed to the fish, some environmentalists in Kazakhstan created sturgeon fish farms to increase supplies. Other activists educated Kazakhs who live near the Caspian about the sea's environment. In response, citizens have formed rescue committees to sustain the sea and its valuable resource. Their efforts may turn a tragic tale into a successful fish story.

As a result, many new political parties are forming, including some with religious programs. Several Muslim parties want the government to declare Kazakhstan an Islamic republic. Ethnic Kazakhs want their country to establish closer ties with Muslim countries, including Iran, Pakistan, Turkey, and Iraq. But many ethnic Russians oppose these policies, and the emigration of Russian workers is hurting Kazakh industries. Before the country can prosper, Kazakhstan's political and ethnic groups must find common ground for cooperation.

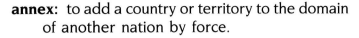

annex: to add a country or territory to the domain of another nation by force.

Autonomous Kirghiz Soviet Socialist Republic: a Kazakh republic founded in 1920 that joined the newly formed Union of Soviet Socialist Republics in 1922. In 1923, this region was renamed the Kazakh Autonomous Republic.

collective farm: a large agricultural estate worked by a group. The workers usually received a portion of the farm's harvest as wages. On a Soviet collective farm, the central government owned the land, buildings, and machinery.

Commonwealth of Independent States: a union of former Soviet republics founded in December 1991. The commonwealth has no formal constitution and functions as a loose economic and military association.

Communist: a person who supports Communism —an economic system in which the government owns all farmland and the means of producing goods in factories.

coup d'état: French words meaning "blow to the state" that refer to a swift, sudden overthrow of a government.

ethnic Kazakh: a person whose ethnic heritage is Turkic and who speaks Kazakh.

ethnic Russian: a person whose ethnic heritage is Slavic and who speaks Russian.

ethnic Slav: a member of an ethnic group that originated in central Asia and that later moved into Russia and eastern Europe.

Hikers enjoy the breathtaking scenery of the Tien Mountains of eastern Kazakhstan.

glasnost: meaning "openness," the Russian name for a policy of easing restrictions on writing and speaking.

industrialize: to build and modernize factories for the purpose of manufacturing a wide variety of consumer goods and machinery.

joint venture: an economic partnership between a locally owned business and a foreign-owned company.

Kazakh Soviet Socialist Republic: a republic of the USSR founded in 1936 with the same borders as modern Kazakhstan.

perestroika: a policy of economic restructuring introduced in the late 1980s. Under perestroika, the Soviet state loosened its control of industry and agriculture and allowed small private businesses to operate.

Russian Empire: a large kingdom that covered present-day Russia as well as areas to the west and south. It existed from roughly the mid-1500s to 1917.

Sharia: a system of laws and customs based on the teachings of the Koran, the Islamic holy book.

steppe: a region of open, level grassland that is suitable for herding livestock and, if rainfall is adequate, for growing crops.

Sufism: a branch of the Islamic faith, whose believers worship in private and follow mystics.

Union of Soviet Socialist Republics (USSR): a large nation in eastern Europe and northern Asia that consisted of 15 member-republics. It existed from 1922 to 1991.

United Nations: an international organization formed after World War II whose primary purpose is to promote world peace through discussion and cooperation.

A Kazakh artwork shows a traditionally dressed woman offering a tray of locally grown fruits.

The roof flap on the inside of a yurt allows fresh air to enter and cooking smoke to escape.

• *Photo Acknowledgments* •

Photographs used courtesy of: pp. 1, 2, 10, 12 (bottom), 16 (top), 24, 32 (bottom), 37, 38, 47 (bottom), 48, 50, 53, 54, © Yury Tatarinov; pp. 5, 17, Tamas Gellert; pp. 6, 9, 46, © Tim Riley; p. 8, Virginia Martin; pp. 12 (top), 22 (top), 44 (left), TASS/SOVFOTO; pp. 13, 18 (top), 19, 28 (bottom), 41 (left), 45, 47 (top), Larry Laukka; pp. 18 (bottom), 36 (left), Judy Klein; p. 20, © Mary Ann Brockman; pp. 21 (top), 22 (bottom), 23 (top left and top right), 26 (left), 29, 31 (top), 33, 35, 40, © Iraj Bashiri; pp. 21 (bottom), 34 (top), 36 (right), 41 (right), 44 (right), NOVOSTI/SOVFOTO; p. 23 (bottom), Cynthia Werner; pp. 26 (right), 34 (bottom), Independent Picture Service; p. 27, William Dirks; p. 28 (top), James Ford Bell Library, University of Minnesota; p. 31 (bottom), RIA-NOVOSTI/SOVFOTO; p. 32 (top), William Mandel; p. 51, Petrossian; p. 55, Marilyn Sanchez. Maps and charts: pp. 14-15, 42-43, J. Michael Roy; p. 16 (bottom), Bryan Liedahl; pp. 30, 50, 52, Laura Westlund.

Covers: (Front and back) © Yury Tatarinov